How to Date Authentically: End the Dating Game and Find Lasting Love
By Sam Whitney
Copyright © 2024 by Sam Whitney
All rights reserved. No part of this book may be reproduced, stored in a retrieval system, or transmitted by any means, electronic, mechanical, photocopying, recording, or otherwise, without prior written permission of the author, except for the inclusion of brief quotations in a review.
ISBN: 978-1-940498-39-3
Published with: IngramSpark "Self-published"
Disclaimer:
This book is a work of nonfiction. The content is intended for informational purposes only. The author and publisher disclaim any liability, loss, or risk incurred as a consequence, directly or indirectly, from the use and application of any of the contents of this book.
Cover Design: Mel Wise Designs (design@melwise.com)
First Edition: 2024
For information about permission to reproduce selections from this book, please contact us at: www.rightorhappybook.com

How to Date Authentically

Sam Whitney

HOW TO DATE
AUTHENTICALLY

Contents

Foreword		1
Introduction		7
1	Being Right or Being Happy	11
2	The World of Right	15
3	The "Right" Story	25
4	Superficially Focused	39
5	Alienating Others	49
6	When Things Go to Plan	57
7	Closing the Book on the World of Right	61
8	The World of Happy	65
9	Step 1: Consider Other People	73
10	Step 2: Be Curious	79
11	Step 3: Be Helpful by Being Straightforward	85
12	How Will I Know?	93
13	Final Thoughts On the World of Happy	101
14	Appendix:	107

To my beautiful wife Lizzie.
I hope you know how much I admire you.

Foreword

The author of this book, Sam Whitney, and I share a passion for bringing groundbreaking ideas to the world of dating. Special thanks to Chris Wallace, who recognized our mutual interests and introduced us. Sam and I began collaborating in September 2017.

For decades I have been intrigued with this exciting, challenging, and confusing world of dating. My passion for this unique moment in the journey of human connection has stayed alive through my 28-year career as a therapist and adjunct professor of positive psychology.

I am also a husband of nearly 30 years and a father of seven children, five of whom are currently dating. I have had them all read this book.

I hold a master's degree in theory and philosophy of psychology and a master's in social work. I even did my master's thesis on a subscale (Family and Home Background) of the Prep-M, a premarital inventory to assess values, perspectives, and priorities in areas shown to be important for marital satisfaction.

As a Licensed Clinical Social Worker, I am writing this foreword to share the joy of this project and a heartfelt desire for happy dating, marriages, families, and future generations. I believe hope and happiness in dating are possible and likely if approached in the ways discussed in this book.

Today's dating culture often emphasizes personal wants, needs, and desires as the guide for dating fulfillment which leads to problems caused by paradigm blindness. This self-focused approach is flawed, as it overlooks the importance of mutual respect, common humanity, and genuine interest in others' hopes and needs. This is pervasive across most of modern psychology. When we work from a self focus for relationship/dating success, it produces a conflict that we can't see but we feel. It invites the other person to also focus on themselves. This creates a paradox wherein our search for self-fulfillment ultimately becomes the very obstacle to its achievement. Carl Jung once said, "The conscious mind...is not always either willing or able to put forth the extraordinary intellectual and moral effort needed to take a paradox seriously."

Consider these statistics:

- Pew Research Center reports that 47% of Americans believe dating is harder now than it was 10 years ago.
- 49% of singles have made recent changes to prioritize themselves. ("Singles in America" by Match, 2023)
- 32% of single men have been rejected because their potential date wanted to focus on themselves (Plenty of Fish, Oct. 4, 2022).
- 80% of 18 to 25-year-olds prioritize their own self-care when dating (Tinder's Future of Dating Report, 2023).

Dating apps and social media are also shifting trends and attitudes. Dr. Carole Lieberman, a Beverly Hills psychiatrist, notes that people are quick to give up on relationships, thinking, "I'll just keep swiping; there's got to be someone who can make me happier."

I firmly believe this book is vital in today's dating landscape. Sam presents a different, liberating, and enlightening view of dating, aiming for peace, fantastic experiences, and dynamic results. It encourages readers to see others as real people and discover genuine, lasting connections. In the short time this book has been in print, it has already improved individuals' dating success, with several people crediting these ideas for their marriages.

Read this book as an exploration and invitation. Approach it with a beginner's mind, remembering that truth is revealed in the living of it. Engage with the experiments, exercises, and challenges presented. Consider it a life landscape evaluation. Trust that it can make a difference for you. Read it periodically and note your discoveries and epiphanies. Honor your senses to be and do.

Sam has a unique gift for sharing in this book. His expertise and experience in working with and living this paradigm, along with his content creation skills, make this book impactful.

NOW IT IS TIME to discover a new way to date, to see, and to consider others and yourself. Read, write, apply, and please share your experiences with us.

- Jason Conover LCSW

"The real voyage of discovery consists not in seeking new landscapes, but in having new eyes." – Marcel Proust

Introduction

"Soooo... how is it going?" my dad asked as he cornered me in the kitchen. "Awesome. Mom makes the best Christmas cookies," I said, as I bit the head off a sprinkle-covered gingerbread man. My dad just looked at me with that expression that said, "that's not what I meant." After a little pause, an eye roll, a sigh, and another cookie (fine, two more), I replied, "Well you know, we've been dating for about a month now and it's going great." My dad then asked, "Do you have a picture of her?" I pulled out my phone. As Facebook loaded, I realized her profile picture wasn't what I was hoping for. Luckily, my sister walked in the door, distracting my dad and buying me a few precious moments to search for a better picture. "How many photos can you take where you don't smile?" I thought to myself, feeling frustrated. I kept scrolling. Family picture, meh. That time at the beach, too silly. Maybe this one with her roommate at the rodeo? Nope! I was really getting desperate now; how hard could it be to find a decent photo of someone? I heard my dad round the corner. I had to choose fast! Just then I found photos of her at her sister's wedding. Her long brown hair was down around her shoulders. Her blue eyes shone beautifully as she smiled. "There she is," I thought to myself. I held up the phone triumphantly. My dad looked at the photo and with a high five said, "Wow, she is really pretty, way to go, man!"

The rest of the night was just like every other Christmas eve: we ate together, watched a movie, and relaxed. But I wasn't relaxed. Something about the photo incident was eating at me. Why had it taken me so long to find a good photo of her? Why couldn't I just show the first photo I had found? I mean, we were dating, and I claimed that the relationship was going well. Was this a sign? Aren't I supposed to be falling in love with this person? Is there something wrong with our relationship? Now I was really in my own head and starting to panic. "Calm down," I thought to myself. "It's not that big of a deal; so what if you took a minute to find a good picture of her, doesn't everyone?"

A few weeks later, we broke up. It seems she wasn't the one. As I did my postmortem relationship analysis, the Facebook picture experience kept coming to mind. What was it about that moment that was so important? The more I thought about it, the more I felt unsettled as I started to see a pattern across all my past dating experiences. I had always assumed that I was single because I hadn't found the right person yet. The truth was that there was another more challenging obstacle to me finding love. An obstacle, as it turns out, that I was responsible for.

I believe I have come to understand what was going on. It was a discovery that transformed my dating experience, led me to marry my wife, and write this book. Let me level with you. The real problem was that while I said I wanted to find true love, marriage and happiness, I was actually up to something else. The Facebook experience revealed that I didn't just want love. I wanted the person I dated to reflect well on me. I was dating to find someone who checked all the right boxes. I was hoping that by finding the best person that my dating journey would be considered a success. In other words, my goal was to be "right" rather than "happy."

I have come to realize that the pursuit of being right is a way of dating and living that is deeply self-focused. It sabotages our ability to be authentic in the dating process and gets in the way of us finding love. In fact, I believe it is one of the key drivers behind dating and relationship dysfunction. In our modern culture, it has infected every aspect of the dating process, turning it into the "game" we have all come to loathe. This book aims to shine a light on the goal of being right. It's also a guide to how to start dating differently if we want to find what I call "happy." We will look at both the world of right and the world of happy to map the terrain for this journey to discover authenticity, end the game, and find lasting love.

Let's begin.

1

Being Right or Being Happy

When I was a kid, I would get in fights with my siblings almost every day. Often my mom would ask me, "Sam, do you want to be right, or do you want to be happy?" Basically, did I want to win an argument at all costs, or was I willing to find a way to work together? This phrase has stuck with me, and I've decided to use it as the framework for describing two very different dating worlds. "Right" and "happy" represent two opposite ways of going about dating. At their core, they are goals that lead to very different results.

Now, when I say goals, you might be thinking about pen and paper lists of aspirations. Or things we want to achieve in the future that are posted to a vision board. This isn't exactly what I mean. When I say the word goal, I mean a desire—a deeply held motivation that orients our choices. Goals at this level are akin to paradigms. They are running in the background like the engine in a car.

These kinds of goals work as filters for incoming information and either amplify or limit what we are able to see. You have likely seen the short video experiment with the basketballs and the gorilla. In the video we see a group of six students passing a ball around. We are told as viewers to count the number of times the ball is passed. As the video comes to a close, we are asked if we saw the large gorilla walking through the scene. Most viewers are astonished to learn that while they were focused on counting the number of passes being made, they completely missed the fact that a large man in a gorilla costume walked right through the group of basketball players. This short example illustrates how our goals can impact what we see. When the goal is to focus on the number of passes, we miss the gorilla walking through the scene. If you were to flip this however and focus on the gorilla, you aren't able to count the passes being made by the players. Our focus determines what information we take in.

Since goals influence how and what we are able to see, our goals also guide behavior. For example, if my goal is to get in shape, then I will begin working out or playing sports to accomplish that goal. If I want to take a trip, I begin planning and saving to make it happen. Whatever they may be, goals help to direct our behavior toward their accomplishment.

When we approach dating with the goal of being right, we are primarily focused on ourselves. We want to find the best possible person to help us bring to life our self-focused vision of happiness. Someone who will ensure that our future is a success. We hold out and sift through people until we find what we deem as worthy of our commitment. In essence we are saying: "When I find the right person, then I will be happy." Even if we are surrounded by excellent people who could be great partners, like the gorilla, we won't see any opportunities that don't align with our goal.

On the other hand, there is the goal of being happy. Being happy is a goal that originates from a genuine interest in other people and is focused on creating authentic connection. Dating becomes an exciting endeavor as we look for the best relationship rather than the best person. Instead of rigid, preconceived notions of happiness, we are open to being surprised. We understand that love is built together; it's not simply a gift magically granted when we find the "right" person.

These two overarching goals, being right and being happy, create very different experiences and outcomes. They each guide our behavior and bring out different parts of ourselves. I want to start by taking a trip to the world of right, explore its depths, and uncover ways it may be affecting our dating destiny.

2

The World of Right

When we date in the world of right, we bring with us a very specific vision of what happiness should look like. This vision is a combination of our own expectations, movies we've seen, books we've read, examples and expectations from others, and some imagination tossed in. Dating with the goal of being right becomes a project to bring this vision to life.

We are also subtly looking for someone who will win us the approval of other people. You could say we are dating with something to prove. We want to prove that we are worthwhile and the kind of person that makes the "right" choice when we choose a partner. It's like we are trying to send a postcard of our happiness to others, saying, "Look how much happier I am!" And now with social media, the pressure to find the "right" person has never been higher. Not only do we have to win the approval of our friends and family but everyone we have ever met since kindergarten. Yikes!

Think back to the story from the introduction to this book. When I was looking for the picture of my then girlfriend, I was fixated on finding a photo of her that won me the approval of my family. I was worried that if I couldn't find the right picture that someone might doubt my dating choices. I became annoyed and even blamed my girlfriend for not having a photo that I deemed worthy. In essence, I was using her to try and prove something about myself.

The Set Up

There were countless times in my dating career when I was set up on a blind date. I tended not to like being set up, but you really can't say no when your mom is asking.

I can remember one instance when I was set up on a blind date by a friend. I was excited as my friend extolled this girl's wonderful qualities. The night of the date arrived. As I knocked on the door and my date opened it, I wasn't happy. She wasn't someone that I found attractive at all. I know that is a shallow thing to say, but it was true. I knew right then that I wasn't going to be interested in a second date.

After the date was over, I remember feeling something strange. I felt insulted by my friend who had set me up. What? Why? It might have been normal to feel let down, or disappointed, but insulted? What was going on? As I reflected further, I realized that I felt this way because of what I thought the date said about me. This is how they saw me? This is the kind of person they felt I would like? I was insulted that they would see me as someone who would date someone like her (horrible, I know).

This is the essence of what it means to live with the goal of being right. I was consumed with the idea that I was a certain type of person who ended up with a certain type of person. This specific person would have all the things I wanted and bestow on me the admiration of others. In my distorted opinion, my date that evening had neither and my fixation on myself ruined what could have been a pleasant evening both for me and for my poor date.

Fear Factor

As we peel back the layers of the need to be right, we discover something interesting: fear. We all wrestle with fear, but in this case our fear is different than what we might expect. We might think that the greatest fear would be something like ending up alone, but it's something very different. Our greatest fear in the world of right is that of settling.

To settle means to lower standards or expectations in order to procure a long-term relationship. What kind of person would we be if we settled? What would other people think of us if they knew we didn't marry the "right" person? How could we stand being forever trapped with someone who we felt we settled for?

I can remember the script running in my head as I dated with a need to be right. "My wife and I are both going to be amazing. Sure, other people can go ahead and settle if they want, but not me. I am going for that gold medal; I am going to find that diamond in the rough and then they'll see. No matter what I have to do or how long it takes I am not going to give up." In the world of right, to date anyone who isn't in line with our self-focused goals is seen as settling, and that feels like failure.

Basically, we are saying "I would rather be right than happy." Let that sit for just a second. When we need to be right, we would rather end up alone than sacrifice our vision of what happiness should be. We can't imagine finding happiness outside of our expectations.

A Matter of Opinion

A close friend of mine—let's call him Mark—told me about a time when he started dating a girl at work. It seemed like a match made in heaven, he was falling head over heels for her and it seemed she was for him. One evening after a movie night, Mark finally had the chance to introduce his new girlfriend to his roommate Jeff. Jeff was a very cool guy and someone that others respected a great deal; his opinion mattered to Mark. After the date, Mark immediately interrogated Jeff. "So, what did you think of her?" he almost yelled. Jeff, much to Mark's astonishment, shrugged his shoulders and said, "she was nice, not the kind of girl I would date though." Mark was dumbstruck. "What did Jeff mean? What kind of girl would

Jeff be dating? What is wrong with my girlfriend? What am I not seeing? Is he trying to say she isn't pretty? Am I dating a loser and don't even know it?!" Mark thought. As he analyzed his relationship with this girl, there didn't seem to be anything wrong, but what if he was missing something!? These horrible questions ate at Mark for a week as he continued to date his then girlfriend. Finally, 5 days after that fateful meeting, Mark decided to break things off. Needless to say, she was stunned and hurt.

Mark was relieved to be free of the constant internal turmoil, but he also felt terrible. He had just ended a relationship on no better grounds than that of his roommate not granting his blessing. Mark was so caught up in the world of right that a simple comment from a friend took apart his entire budding romance in under a week. Mark couldn't bear the thought that he was somehow dating someone that wasn't objectively desirable. He was consumed with the fear that he was settling and missing out on the "right" one.

Why We Live in the World of Right

As we explore the caverns of the world of right, some questions might start coming to mind. Why would anyone ever date this way? How do we get here in the first place?

One answer comes from our culture. Dr. C. Terry Warner said, "We all learn to become persons by adopting the practices, the language, the institutions, the emotional repertoire of our people. We become persons by becoming one of them. This repertoire, linguistic, emotional and psychological, includes measures of worth and success and respectability that we aim to feel and by which we judge ourselves, and one another.... These may be the family we belong to, or the wealth we have, or our style, our appearance, our accent, our education, our looks." [I would add whom we choose to date and marry.] Dr. Warner concludes, "So each of us is trying to save himself or herself by measuring up, by arranging ourselves in the minds of other people" (Warner, 2001). In other words, our self-focused goal is shaped by our participation in our culture. We piece together our vision through media, both film and online, and through the stories others tell us about how romance should go. From a young age we are fed a steady diet of narratives which contain requirements that must be met if our romance is to be deemed "authentic" and "real." These narratives tell us that if our relationship meets these requirements, then our future marriage will be a smashing success. If we don't question these sources, we can easily let these crowd-sourced goals direct our lives.

Shopping

When we live in the world of right, dating seems like a problem to be solved. How can I find someone to join me in my pursuit of validation and protect me against relationship failure? In order to solve this problem, we apply a problem-solving framework from another part of our lives. We try to approach dating like we do shopping.

Let's take the example of buying a car. When we go to buy a car, we first come up with a vision of the car we want. We then select cars by weighing their pros and cons against our budget. We hope to find the best deal and maximize the return on our investment.

Think further about when you look for something you want to buy online. I don't know about you, but when I search for something, I tend to ask Google to find me the "best" thing. I often look at reviews and blogs to ensure that I am buying something other people have said is a good idea because I am hoping to avoid mistakes.

Have you ever bought something and then regretted it? Maybe you did all your research only to find that the thing you thought you were buying turned out to be wrong. Buyer's remorse is very real and something we all try to avoid. Each of us has seen bad relationships, broken engagements, horrible marriages, and messy divorces. We are all very much aware of the risks and the high stakes when it comes to dating. We are, after all, trying to make one of the most important decisions of our lives. I believe that our transactional way of dating when we need to be right is often fueled by an idea that if we can just find the right person who checks the boxes then maybe we can avoid relationship failure.

However, the challenge is that when we treat dating like shopping, we are neglecting something fundamental: the fact that we are dealing with people and not objects. When we buy something, we have full control over the process. We get to pick out what we want and if it doesn't work, we can just return it and keep searching. When we are dating, we enter a co-creative process with the other person who has their own inner life and their own agency. However, if we view people as objects, how can we expect to form a lasting and healthy relationship with them? Our dating life, instead of being a chance to connect and cultivate love, becomes a frenzied attempt to seduce the "right person" to reinforce our self-focused project.

Now imagine everyone else running around dating in the world of right. Each person guarding their heart until they find that special someone. People holding back their feelings, selectively communicating, hiding their authentic selves, trying to manipulate each other into fulfilling their own dreams of happiness. Sound familiar? This is what the modern dating "game" looks like. The need to be right creates a culture of dating competition instead of relationship collaboration. It needs to stop.

In summary, our need to be right comes in large part from our need to feel validated and our desire to mitigate possible failures. Both lead us to believe that if only we can find the right person, then we will discover relationship bliss.

You might be wondering if you have been living in the world of right. It can be hard to uncover our deeper goals when we have been living with them for so long. Like fish, it can be difficult to see the water we are swimming in. We have found that there are clues in common experiences that will help us identify this self-focused way of living and root it out. These common experiences take the form of roadblocks, barriers, or symptoms that once we see them can indicate that we might be living in the world of right.

There are three very common experiences that go hand in hand in the world of right. They are:

1. We tell a particular story.
2. Our focus becomes superficial.
3. We alienate the people we are trying to attract.

We will take a deeper look at each one and as we do, I invite you to take a look at yourself and see if any of them apply to you.

3

The "Right" Story

Imagine your life is a play. If you live in the world of right, you are both author and central character of this play—everyone else merely plays a supporting role. With the finished script in hand, you hold auditions as you sift through the masses to find the lucky person to play the role of the love interest in your story.

The Structure of a Great Story

Every great story has a structure, or a way that it is told. Stories have narrative, settings, plots, characters, ideas, conflict, emotion, and resolution. Stories are massively important because we not only tell stories, we live them. We live our daily lives and make our daily choices in line with our story.

When my goal is to be right, my life becomes entangled in the gravitational pull of the story I am living. I am at the center and others simply orbit around me.

My late grandfather knew something about this concept. When he was in first grade, he wrote his name in the middle of a paper and drew a circle around it. On the circle he wrote the word *family*. Then he drew a bigger circle around the smaller one. This next circle read *town*. He drew a bigger circle and labeled it *state*. As you probably guessed, he drew another circle and wrote the word *country*. This pattern continued, with each circle getting bigger and each label detailing a larger mass upon which my grandfather existed, eventually extending to the planet, solar system, galaxy, and UNIVERSE! My grandfather had literally drawn himself at the center of the universe. When our goal is to be right, we are at the center of our own universe and our story becomes very one-sided.

A One-Sided Story

One night, a roommate returned from a date and collapsed on the couch, letting out an exacerbated groan while burying his face in pillows. Being the sensitive and concerned men we were, we gathered around to hear his sad tale. "Uggh, she wasn't interesting at all," he bemoaned. "She didn't get any of my jokes," he complained, "She didn't even like where we went to eat! Who doesn't like PIZZA!?" Then one of my roommates asked, "Was there anything you liked about her?" He thought for a second and told us that she was pretty and played basketball. Those were the only positive things he could tell us about her. Everything else was about how she was not the person he was looking for.

Rude? Yes. However, his telling of this story revealed what he was committed to on this date. He was telling us a self-focused story and omitting many potentially important details about this girl. I'm sure this girl had many wonderful qualities beyond what was described, but those were the only things he could see in her. She wasn't fully a person to him; she wasn't being painted in 3 dimensions. He had judged her unworthy of his further attention. He had not taken the time to learn important things about her. She may have even told him interesting things, but he wasn't paying attention. He noticed only the cosmetic details that interested *him*.

Stop! Does having a bad date mean we are living with the goal of being right, or whatever? Yes and no. It's perfectly possible to have a bad date. We aren't going to match with everyone and sometimes friction can't be helped. However, what I am saying is that when we need to be right, the narrative we are committed to blinds us. So, while the date might have been bad, I would argue that my roommate could have had a much better experience had he not been so fixated on what *he* wanted. He could have been present and open to another person. Who knows, maybe he missed the opportunity to connect with someone.

This one-sided story not only deceives others, but us as well. Our self-focused narrative hides from us something important: that the other person has their own story. We seem to forget this very simple truth and without realizing it, we slip into the belief that our story is the only one. I am the main character, the hero, and others serve only as a supporting role. We become blind to the reality of other people.

Not My Crowd

I took a family sociology class in college—a very crowded family sociology class. One day, the professor announced that, statistically speaking, more than half of us would marry and have kids sometime in the next decade. As I thought about this, I looked around the room filled with people, most of them women my age. The thought came to me: half of the girls in this room would marry men that found them beautiful and wonderful. Yet I didn't think of these girls as people I wanted to take on a date, let alone marry. I had been in the class for two months and had ample time to observe them. What was I not seeing? Why had I judged them not worthy of my affections?

I would argue that I hadn't seen them because I was blind. None of the girls in my class were people that I felt were going to be part of my story. The reason was because of the school I was attending at the time. You see, I had been forced, due to my poor academic performance, to attend the local public university instead of the more prestigious private university in the same town. I had tried several times to get into the other university and after failing had decided to enroll in public. I felt embarrassed to be attending the college because in my mind it was a place for people who couldn't cut it in the "big leagues." This meant that when attending classes I was thinking that the girls at that school were beneath me in some way. I was just there biding my time until I could transfer and so I wanted to wait until that happened to seriously date. I was telling myself a story about who I thought I was—someone better than the people in my school—and a story about these girls not being worth my time. My way of seeing was blinding me to the truth about these people and blocking potential connections I might have made. I couldn't see the wonderful and amiable qualities other men would someday see.

I invite you to consider whether you have ever dated with the blindness of the need to be right. Seriously, put down this book and think for a moment about your last date. What stands out to you about the person you were on a date with? Were you focused on only the faults of this person or their strengths as well? Can you recall things about them that interested you as well as things that did not, or was your experience one-sided? Can you remember things about them that didn't apply to what you were looking for? These can be hard questions. However, they can help us to identify our focus when we are with others.

The Plot Thickens

An important aspect of any good story is that of the plot. As we develop the plot for our story, we want it to be compelling. We work to shape the setting and events of the story so that when the moment of true love arrives, the audience will swoon. At the end of the day, we are trying to get things to play out in just the right way.

I have a friend who, after reading this book, told me about how he was holding himself back because of the story he was telling. Early on in his dating journey, my friend (let's call him Jordan) had it in his head that he was going to find someone to marry while traveling the world. He didn't know all the details, just that he was going to be somewhere exotic, maybe doing charity work, and his future wife was going to be on the same project, or something like that. They would meet and almost instantly hit it off and then date and get married shortly after. Maybe a destination wedding and an even cooler honeymoon would come with it. Basically, a Hallmark movie.

While you might be laughing with Jordan about this, the fact is that he had a pre-set idea of how his dating story was going to play out. He told me that it blocked him from pursuing other avenues to find love. He didn't feel a lot of traction in traditional dating as he was holding out for this special and very specific story to be realized. He told me as well that he especially didn't want to do any online dating. Jordan said that he didn't have anything against online dating, it was just not how his story was going to go. He didn't want to be one of those guys who met his wife online.

The good news is that after reading this book, Jordan reported that he felt inspired to question his story. He figured that if he was really committed to finding happiness, he needed to be proactive and not wait for his fantasy travel story to unfold. He decided right then to open an online dating profile on a popular dating app. Lo and behold, the first girl he matched with is now his wife. (*Please expect this to happen to you instantly. Drop this book and start online dating... jk.)

My good friend, we will call her Kylie, offered to share her experience with us. Kylie told me that for as long as she can remember she yearned for a Pride-and-Prejudice style dating story. It was, after all, her favorite movie. She would play the part of the witty and beautiful damsel, waiting for her perfect, handsome, well established "Mr. Darcy" to arrive. Brimming with confidence, he would profess his love without reserve. He would make it clear that he would do anything for her. Right from the beginning, there would exist an effortless connection. She admitted that her story was one where she didn't have to do very much. Love was supposed to just come into her life.

As Kylie was basking in this dream, she started a new job working at a local elementary school. She just so happened to start on the same day as another new, and cute, employee named Ryan. A few weeks later, daily chatting gave way to hanging out and eventually dating. Everything seemed to be going just as Kylie had planned. That was until Kylie discovered that Ryan had been married before. "What!? He's divorced!? What does that mean? Does that matter? Should that matter? Can I trust him? What am I going to tell other people? This wasn't supposed to happen! Am I horrible for thinking these things?!" were some of the about 1 million thoughts and insecurities that ran through her head. Kylie began to realize that her story wasn't playing out like she had hoped. Instead of the idealized character she had imagined, Ryan didn't feel a sense of worth after his divorce, and he didn't feel he could trust himself to find happily ever after. He was telling himself a story filled with deep shame. He wasn't in a state to play Mr. Darcy to Kylie's Ms. Bennet.

When Kylie reflected with me on this experience, she recalled how she wrestled with her story. Should she continue dating Ryan? Or, should she wait and hope that a new Mr. Right would find his way to her? One thing was clear. If it was going to work with Ryan, she needed to throw her story out the window and play a different role. That is exactly what she did. She let go of her preconceived notions and chose to see Ryan as a person. Kylie took time to learn about who he was. This included being honest and asking hard questions as she worked through her own feelings. She came to trust him, and that helped to rekindle his self-confidence. Her approach gave him the hope of a fun and loving relationship, enough to throw out his own story of being unworthy of love and accept real love for the first time. If Kylie had allowed her story to win the day, she wouldn't now be happily married to Ryan with a rambunctious baby girl.

Requiring that our story play out in the "right" way only limits our future happiness. We are blocked from seeing potential in others. We are also blocked from bringing our authentic selves into the dating process as we hold out for the story to be right. When we rigidly hold to the plot, we aren't allowing for the creative process of relationship building to get underway. We need to make space for surprise, allowing what might seem mundane to flower into something special.

Feel-Good Feature Film

A core feature of any great romantic tale is that of passion. Strong, vibrant, emotional infatuation is something we all expect when we hear a great love story. Feeling in love, enamored, and twitterpated are all important feelings for a successful romance. The challenge is that when we need to be right, we prioritize these feelings above all else. We yearn for them because they signal to us and to others that we have found the right person, we are telling the right story and that we've made the right choice. Right?

In our misguided fixation on our feelings, we mistake chemistry for connection as our excitement at finding someone to compliment our story overshadows what really matters. Our need to be right distorts our perceptions and therefore impacts our feelings in a way that makes them unreliable. We then, in turn, place undue pressure on these feelings to be our guides. If it weren't for the need to be right messing with the order of operations, our feelings would come as a welcome support to a healthy and budding romance. Instead, they arrive like a tidal wave to wipe out any potential red flags.

It's a Trap!

Fixating on our stories and prioritizing our enamored feelings leads us into a trap: we start to believe that falling in love isn't something we are responsible for. It's the other person's job to bring love into our lives. "When I meet them, I'll just know." This is a seductive idea because as I hold out for serendipity, I get to neglect my responsibility to find love. All I need to do is wait for someone that will simply make me want to commit.

Nothing keeps us from finding happiness more than not taking responsibility for its achievement, especially in dating. As we refuse to act and create the conditions wherein love might grow, our frustration grows instead, and so do our excuses.

I know this was true of me. I was great at avoiding my responsibility for love. My dad eventually called me the "Jerry Seinfeld" of dating, as I was constantly coming up with ways to explain why I was single and why the girls I dated were falling short. I was waiting for the right feeling to come along and flip the switch for me. I didn't want to put my heart on the line even though I was asking the girls I was dating to do that very same thing.

Falling Hard and Fast

Before we close this chapter, I want to share with you a story that I feel sums up what we have been talking about. It's a story about how my own need to be right got me dumped. Buckle up.

A couple of years before I got married, I reconnected with someone who I had met during college and I fell hard and fast. I couldn't sleep because I lay awake at night thinking about her. I would go on runs past her apartment hoping to run into her. I started having a hard time concentrating at work. I was a wreck, and I loved it. I had finally found what I had been looking for! Best part, she even liked me back. We started going out and things picked up quickly, or so I thought.

I can remember one date we went on where I tried to hold her hand, and she didn't let me. I thought to myself, "That's weird, maybe she doesn't want to date me?" I squashed that thought with, "Naw, she just isn't a person who likes to hold hands all the time." There were other times when she was hard to get a hold of and I would say to myself, "She must be so busy with work; how cool that she is so dedicated." You can probably see where this relationship was going, but I can tell you I didn't. After a month, everything suddenly ended. She didn't want to date anymore. I was baffled and completely heartbroken. What had gone wrong? Why had I fallen into something that turned out to be false?

Looking back, the answer is pretty clear: I fell hard and fast because the story made sense. She reinforced my idea that I was the kind of guy who ended up with a girl like her. She made me feel validated as a person. My guy friends were jealous, and the girls I hung out with hated her. Before the breakup, I remember thinking, "Finally, this is the person I have been waiting for! All of this dating garbage has been worth it." I was sure that life would be smooth sailing from then on.

I was filled with what I imagined were all the right emotions to have. I felt that I could trust these feelings and charge blindly into the relationship with the promise of my story taking its next logical step toward happiness. I was wrong. My feelings deceived me and caused me to conflate attraction and infatuation with love. I made excuses as I attempted to force a relationship back to life that had never really gotten started.

When I got dumped, I found all sorts of ways to spin the story to shift responsibility away from me. I would tell people it was because she was from California and girls there are just shallow. Or I would say that we just weren't on the same page on the "important stuff." I was also prone to say that she was just crazy and since she was so pretty that she had to be extra crazy. Regardless of the story I chose, each one had a goal in mind: to excuse me for failing to capture what was supposed to be the lifelong romance I had lived for.

As I reflect now, I can see that I was experiencing the need to be right. For example, I wasn't really listening on our dates and when we did talk, I was caught up in my own head trying to come up with something to say. I constantly worried about what she was thinking. I was scared to death that she was going to wake up and realize that she could do way better than me. I would have told you I was thinking about her, but I wasn't. I was scheming about how I could get her to stay. I wasn't able to be my authentic self in our relationship because I was trying to be who I thought she wanted me to be. I guarantee you she did not feel a desire to commit to me because she could tell I wasn't really in love with her. I was in love with the idea of her with me.

Our allegiance to living out the right story is strong. It can dictate how we date, who we date, and why we are even dating in the first place. Identifying and coming to terms with our stories is important if we want to extricate ourselves from the world of right. Later, we will look at ways we can turn the dial down on our own stories and become far more interested in others. For now, let's take a look at our second but equally self-sabotaging roadblock, being superficially focused.

4

Superficially Focused

Now that we have our story written, it's time to go and find someone to cast as the main love interest in our tale. During each audition, or date, we are looking to find qualities that match what we think would make us happy. We latch on to people who appear to fulfill our vision; we are easily put off by those who fall short of our ideal. We are focused on what can most easily prove our value and justify our dating choices—the outward appearance and characteristics of the other person.

For Science

Several years ago, a friend and some research colleagues set up an experiment to see just how fixated we have become on outward appearance when it comes to dating. His group created a fake online dating profile using photos of a former Miss USA. The profile consisted of five photos, a little bio and no additional information. It obviously screamed SCAM!

After creating the profile, the team went to work connecting with as many local guys as they could. Given the obviously sketchy looking profile they had made, they thought no one would take them seriously. The next morning, they were shocked to see that the profile had netted over 200 connections.

Blown away by the success of their initial experiment, the group decided to take things a step further. They spent the better part of a day sending the same message to all of the connections they had just made. The message instructed each guy that our fake girl was going to be at a local frogurt (frozen yogurt) shop that Friday at 9 p.m.

The fateful night arrived. The team didn't think anyone would actually show up, but as the clock struck 9, cars full of guys began arriving at the frogurt shop. One source reported that over 70 guys arrived to meet this mystery girl. There they were, standing around, lining the walls of the shop, all holding their breath to have the chance to date a fake supermodel. It wasn't until someone had the guts to speak up that the group realized they had been catfished.

This story is entertaining, but the social experiment reveals a deeper truth about our dating culture. The fact that 70 guys actually showed up at a frogurt shop based solely on a photograph and an obviously less-than-legit profile is alarming. For these guys, the goal seems to have been finding an attractive partner at any cost.

You might be thinking, "Yeah, men are the worst, and this is not a surprising story; this is how it's been since the dawn of time." And I agree to an extent. That being said, pursuing an attractive partner isn't bad in and of itself, and most healthy romances have a generous amount of attraction. However, I would argue that when we need to be right, we have an added motivation beyond our natural desire to be with an attractive person. Our story drives us to prioritize a person's outward appearance over anything else.

More Than Good Looks

Now, lest you think that outward appearance only means good looks, there are other forms of attractiveness that drive this singular fixation when we need to be right. We might be focused on someone's money, their job title, their clothing, their car or motorcycle, or their major in school; or we might be focused on if they are intellectual, musical, well-traveled, well-read... and the list goes on. These qualities might make up part of what draws us toward someone, but when we need to be right these qualities consume our search and drive us to ignore other positive and negative qualities in a person.

Our superficial focus is not entirely due to our need to be right. We want to find a partner who is attractive to us. The problem is when it is the *most important* quality we look for in a person. I believe being overwhelmingly fixated on outward appearances is driven by the need to be right. After all, we don't just want to find someone we are attracted to—we want someone by our side who helps earn us the approbation of others.

My friend and neighbor in college, we will call her Emily, had a fascinating dating experience that provides a deeper look at what we have been talking about. Emily was an accounting major and had planned to attend the end of the year event for the business school. Of course, she had to invite her boyfriend, we will call him Jack, and she was excited for her colleagues to meet him. However, her plan hit a snag when Jack showed up to her door looking, in her words, "like a total goober." Emily said that "he looked like a 15-year-old going to his first party. Imagine a cross between Justin Bieber and a Bible salesman, somehow his shirt made him look even shorter!" Needless to say, it wasn't a good look. Emily says that she was so disappointed by how he looked that she lost all interest in going to the event and invited him out for ice cream instead. She was horrified by the thought that the people at the business school would see them together and question why she was dating him. In short, at that moment, Emily was embarrassed of him. As Emily reflected with me on the experience, she was shocked at how she had reacted. After all, it wasn't that different from how he would have normally dressed. Emily says that they had been dating pretty seriously and that they had even talked about getting engaged in the near future. What is so interesting is that in the face of potentially looking bad in front of her friends, Emily's goal of being right was revealed. She was focused completely on the outward appearance of her boyfriend and what others would think if they were seen together.

What is funny is that the next week they went to a reunion for a church mission. Emily and Jack had actually met as missionaries for their church the year before. He had been a leader in the mission and someone that others looked up to. When the time came for them to go to the reunion, she was excited to go with him. The people at this reunion knew and even revered him. This evening was a chance for Emily to show off that she had gotten "that" guy. As they made the rounds holding slices of pizza, Emily was grinning ear to ear as person after person commented, "Oh my gosh, you guys are dating, that is amazing, you guys are perfect together!" What a great night, right?

These stories are very interesting as they show us how powerful the need to be right can be. Emily was deeply concerned with how who she dated reflected on how other people saw and judged her. Her level of attraction to her then boyfriend would come and go depending on who they would be meeting. She was superficially focused and craved the validation of others.

My wife, Liz, told me recently that when we first started dating, there were superficial things that I lacked that held her back from dating me exclusively. I wasn't very musical (she plays three instruments), I didn't like roller coasters (she's an adrenaline junkie), and I wasn't planning on becoming a doctor (she was studying to be a nurse). At the time, Liz was seeing what I was rather than who I was. I was not fitting in the mold she had prefabricated when she came to our relationship. It took time for her to realize that I was more than just the lack of superficial aspects she was focusing on.

Never Say Never

Our superficial focus goes beyond a carefully curated list of things we want in a future partner. There is another side of the coin I like to call the "nope list." These are qualities that if discovered in a potential partner are grounds for terminating the relationship. When we need to be right, the items on our nope list are different from what are real deal breakers. A real deal breaker would be "I won't date someone I can't trust," or "I don't date people who won't respect my boundaries." From the need to be right, the nope list looks more like, "I don't date people who like video games" or "I won't go out with someone who loves country music" or "I don't date people who don't go to the gym." The nope list when we need to be right are items that are calculated to ensure that we don't end up with someone who might embarrass us.

Interestingly, I found that often people are willing to sacrifice something on their must have list like "plays a musical instrument" or "going to be a doctor" in the name of love and connection. However, I very rarely see people willing to cross anything off their nope list. These items seem immovable because to allow any of them would be in direct violation of the need to be right. Now, again, there are real deal breakers. We need to be aware that to break away from the world of right does not mean we lower our standards of integrity. We want to hold the line when it comes to things like boundaries, trust, and equality in our relationships. The challenge is when we have real deal breakers confused with items that are simply on our self-focused nope list.

Have you ever done a Google search for something very specific, but you put in too many search criteria? If you have tried this, you have likely seen how Google has a hard time presenting options to you. This is because the search criteria are too narrow. It is only when we remove some of the seemingly important criteria that the search engine is able to produce more helpful options. The same goes for dating. Holding too hard to our needs list or our nope list narrows our focus too much. It makes it hard to find anyone who can satisfy what we want and avoid what we don't. By critically thinking about our lists, we can eliminate items that are just about being right and keep the things that are essential.

Before we move on, I want to take a minute to address the idea of a true deal breaker a bit more. What if someone has a difficult past, challenging family dynamics, addiction of any kind, or has been married before, to name a few. These might be real deal breakers for you. But maybe not. There is no right or wrong answer here and I offer no specific advice. When it comes to these more personal criteria for choosing to date someone, I suggest you follow the steps outlined in the last half of this book. They will help you to analyze and decide for yourself what makes sense and if something should or should not be a true deal breaker.

Next time you encounter something that seems to be on your nope list, just think for a moment, is this something that is a real deal breaker? Or is this something that is simply different than what you would do? Don't let the nope list derail you from finding someone you could really be happy with.

Mirror, Mirror

Our focus on the superficial doesn't just apply to others, it works on us as well. This fixation on the external bleeds into our own mirror and we can't help but become more critical of our reflection. When we need to be right, we become overly concerned with our physical appearance and accomplishments. When this occurs, I have seen a couple of things happen.

#1: Our obsession with the external leads us to feel anxious and worried as we wonder if we are enough. This, in turn, only serves to inflame our insecurities and make dating more difficult. You might have been told that we can't love others until we love ourselves. I believe this isn't quite right. We might be able to express love to others even without self-love, but without it we aren't capable of receiving love. How can we allow another person to love us when we are feeling that we are not lovable? Our focus on the superficial fools us into thinking that if we don't possess the right looks or qualities then we are not worthy of love. This makes connection impossible and dating difficult.

#2. We respond to our insecurities not with defeat but with action. We work hard to look good and have enough lofty accomplishments that others will simply fall for us. And it works!

The problem? This strategy only works in the short term. Our superficial focus only attracts those with a superficial focus, and this leaves us disappointed and frustrated as we find ourselves dating those who don't really love us for who we are.

The Danger of Comparison

One of the most dangerous aspects of having a superficial dating focus is that of comparison. Nothing will ruin a relationship more quickly than that of comparing it to another. When we see only the superficial, we tend to compare what others have to what we don't have. Others' happiness seems to take away from our own.

Let's say that we encounter someone who in some way is more attractive to us than the person we are currently dating. If our goal is to maximize our happiness and validation, we might start to wonder what it might be like to find someone even more attractive. As this thought grows, it draws us away from the person we are pursuing in order to pursue something else. I say "something," because remember, neither the person we are dating nor the "better" option we have found are really people to us. They are simply interchangeable pieces in our lives. When we date in this way, we fall into a trap of a never-ending search for better prospects. We resist the pull of commitment, because to stop looking would be to cut off our options.

This problem of comparison has only been exacerbated by the internet and social media. Thanks to social media, we can compare ourselves to others at any moment. We have even built dating apps that allow us to see better prospects at the swipe of our fingertips. This technology has created a way for us never to be truly connected to one person as we look to be more and more connected to many people. This leads us to judge others more for their profile picture than for who they really are.

Our need to be right drives us to live a story that distorts what we look for while dating. We find ourselves fixated on the outward appearance of others and allow it to drive our dating decisions. This leads us to limit our options and fall into the trap of comparison.

If you haven't noticed already, we have been very much focused in the first part of this book on the need to be right and its impact on ourselves. However, there is another side to the dating coin that is often forgotten: the other person. Let's dive in now and explore what it's like to date someone living in the world of right.

5

Alienating Others

For most of this book, we have been looking at what it's like to be someone with a need to be right. However, have you considered what it might be like to be the other person in this equation? The love interest of someone with the need to be right. What is it like to be seen as a chess piece and moved around without much say in the matter? What is it like to be ignored because you don't fit the mold? How about being pursued only because you fit into the narrative as someone's love interest with them as the hero of the story? For this next chapter let's flip things around and look at how our need to be right impacts those we are trying to date.

The fact is, people are very perceptive to how others feel about them. Think about your family, your coworkers, and your friends. You know which people in these groups like you the most and which ones simply tolerate you. Have you ever been around someone who was nice to you because they wanted something? How about someone who harbored secret distaste for you? Or someone who was in love with you but never said something? In each instance, you probably sensed the way the other person felt about you, even if he or she never openly said it.

When we are with someone who needs to be right, we can feel it. It's like they aren't there with us. They aren't really listening to or seeing us. It's like we are there in support of their experience and we never get to share the spotlight. It isn't a great place to be, and it definitely doesn't inspire connection and long-term commitment.

Regardless of our charm, charisma, good looks, sense of humor, or other external qualities, those we date know how we feel about them deep down. Our self-focused way of seeing alienates the very people we are trying to attract.

Persistent Jerry

When my wife, Liz, was single, she was pursued by a guy named Jerry. Jerry was good-looking, established, musical, and very friendly. He was also interested in dating Liz very soon after they met. However, Liz quickly began to suspect that she couldn't trust Jerry. After all, he'd wanted to date her before he even knew her very well. She could tell that Jerry wasn't really interested in *her*—he was just chasing her for selfish ends. She turned down her would-be suitor.

But the story didn't end there. Jerry simply wouldn't take "no" for an answer. Although Jerry had agreed to Lizzie's request that they just be friends, he was always trying to get her to date him. Watching a movie? He would try to cuddle with her. Out for a walk? Time to confess his love. Regardless of how clearly Liz expressed her disinterest in dating him, he wouldn't relent. Even when Liz was seriously dating me, Jerry was still trying.

What fascinates me about this story is how stubborn Jerry was when it came to dating Liz. No matter what she said or how she said it, he was still in pursuit. He was unable to see how his behavior alienated her. In his mind, he probably thought that she was just scared or that she really liked him and just needed a push in the right direction. He likely thought that he was making all the right moves to draw her in. However, his self-focused attitude blocked him from connecting with Liz. Although he had many of the qualities she was looking for, the way he saw Liz ultimately drove her away.

Sadly, this story is all too common. Jerry is just one example of how our need to be right can impact those we want to date. Because we aren't really seeing them, we often struggle to understand them. And, once again, we become frustrated as we are unable to find lasting connection.

No Rest 'Til Right

My friend and colleague, Jason, had a fascinating experience while dating a girl that revealed his own need to be right. Here is the story in his own words.

"I was in college and dating a nice girl named Karen. We had been going out for 1–2 months and things seemed to be going quite well. I felt she was my type and it seemed we were getting along nicely. Then one evening we were at her apartment and she said, "You are not really my type." "What?!," I thought. My mind exploded. It was all pretty surreal. I asked her what her type was, and she said something about dark hair and other features. I failed to accept. Because I saw Karen as my type, I was hugely biased towards me being her type. It is crazy how this happened—needing to be right made me so oblivious to the obvious. It gets worse. For the next 6 hours I continued to attempt to convince Karen that I was right. I am not sure how I could have talked about it for that long. I know one thing: she was saintly in her patience and in her maintaining her position. It was starting to get light when I left her apartment feeling like a dog with its tail between its legs."

I can feel for Jason. His need to be right drove him to do something completely counterproductive to his goal. What's even more interesting is that his need to be right became so literal. The sad part is that it was only after this experience that Jason realized how crazy he had been. That's the weird thing about the need to be right. It blinds us to how our feelings and behavior are alienating others. This means that when we date this way, we end up disappointed and we don't even have a clue as to the source.

In the movie *500 Days of Summer* the main character, Tom, is devastated after the love of his life, Summer, dumps him without warning. As he reflects on their relationship and tells others about it, all he can recount is how wonderful Summer was, how happy he felt, and how hopeless things were.

At a key moment in the movie, Tom's sister tells him to remember negative things along with the positive. When Tom does this, he is astounded to discover that Summer had been checked out of the relationship for months. On top of that, they had constantly fought and Tom hadn't even noticed. Tom had been so focused on the idea that he and Summer were going to end up together that he had completely glossed over the issues that had sunk their relationship.

In this case, Tom was so keen on making the relationship work that he couldn't see the experience Summer was, or wasn't, having. His attempts to revive the relationship only pushed Summer further away and blocked him from understanding the source of the relationship dysfunction.

Masks

When we are caught up in our stories and trying to seduce another person to join our quest for happiness, we aren't able to bring forward an authentic version of ourselves. We feel a bit fake, like we are putting on a show. Each date means a new mask to try on and a new way to get someone to like us. It is exhausting dating in the world of right because we are always spending energy adjusting to endear ourselves to the "right" kind of people. Instead of being relaxed, open, and true to who we are, we find ourselves contorted and/or with a feeling of disconnection. Other people can sense this in us. They can feel that we aren't being truthful. Others aren't likely to want to connect with us for the long term if we aren't able to show them who we are deep down.

For me, this struggle with authenticity took the form of being a "Nice Guy." I was always willing to bend over backwards to help and accommodate others. I had absolutely no boundaries and would never impose. I thought I was being a good person and that if I was nice and helpful girls would like me. It turns out they only saw me as immature and indecisive. What's worse, when I was out with someone I was attracted to, I would extend awkward compliments, feel anxious, and/or be overly chivalrous as my nervous brain would spit out any strategy to get them to like me. I couldn't see the impact of what I was doing. "It looks like nice guys finish last!" I would exclaim as I chalked up my rejections to girls not liking nice guys. The truth was that being a nice guy wasn't the problem, it was being a fake version of a nice guy. I don't know of anyone who wouldn't want someone who was kind and helpful. The problem was that I wasn't truly interested in the girls I was trying to date. I was caught up in my need to impress. The girls I pursued could sense this in me and eventually would see through me. I wasn't able to see how my "Nice Guy" act was getting in the way of what I wanted.

Among the many negative side effects of the need to be right, our tendency to alienate others is the most devastating. We drive the people we want away as we approach them with only ourselves in mind. We even run the risk of inviting into our lives those we don't like, or worse, those who are bad for us. Only when we are able to set ourselves free from the goal of being right can we begin to attract the best relationship into our lives. Only then will we create the fertile ground upon which the seeds of love can grow and, more importantly, thrive.

6

When Things Go to Plan

You might be reading this book and thinking: how in the world can we ever find love and connection with the goal of being right blocking our every effort? I want to tell you something that may surprise you. The need to be right isn't dangerous simply because it blocks our success in dating. It's dangerous because sometimes the story we create when we need to be right comes true.

When we succeed in the world of right, we find someone who fits the bill, compliments our story, looks great, and gives us all the validation we have been craving. Our emotions and passions are right there to help us, and we feel like we are moving in the right direction. The other person gets what they want as well, we match their story and validate their need to be right. It's especially exciting because of the big wedding and the outpouring of support our relatives are obligated to shower upon us. All of this can shroud a truth that we might not be fully aware of, that our relationship is built on shaky ground.

Imagine what it would be like to be married in the world of right. Take all of the ideas we have been talking about and stretch them out over a lifelong relationship. The other person has been placed into our production to play a specific part in an ever-evolving story. We are all familiar with the prenuptial agreement, a contract that particularly shrewd couples enter into in order to pre-empt the divorce proceedings. When we marry with a need to be right, it's like we've signed an unseen behavioral prenuptial agreement. In essence we have said that we will be happy insofar as the other person holds up their end of the bargain. They have to reinforce my story by validating me, stay vibrant and attractive, and bend to my will for our future plans.

What happens when the other person changes, or we change? What happens to the passion, desire, fun, and connection we thought we had? How about when the other person stops reinforcing our story or neglects our wants? What happens when the truth that they are a person full of gross habits and their own problems comes to light? What do we do when our significant other embarrasses us or refuses to conform to our will for something like finances, intimacy, or children? How do we cope when the primary purpose of this person was to play a part and they go off script? How about when we run into other people who are more attractive than our partner or a better "fit" in our story? In many cases our feelings go from excited to resentful. We move from connection to feelings of isolation. We fall back on the habits of blame and finger pointing to console ourselves. In essence what we are saying is, "If only I had married the right person, then I would be happy." Even from the safe harbor of a relationship we still hear the siren's call to something better.

Let's say that you are able to survive the initial shock of finding out that you married an imperfect mortal. From the need to be right, we don't move from acceptance to love, we simply reallocate our efforts to find validation in our marriage to other pursuits. Maybe we bury ourselves in our work or pursue money and toys. Maybe we find our passion in travel and trips at the expense of our family. It could take the form of immersing ourselves in the kids and ignoring our spouse. Perhaps a project or our community is where we will find our prominence. Whatever form it takes, our need to be right, if not cured or at least mitigated can compel us to find validation in other arenas, leaving us to neglect our most important relationship.

If you are reading this and realizing that you might be in a relationship touched by the need to be right, fear not. Needing to be right is not our default setting or an unbreakable mindset that has us trapped forever. Realizing we are living with the need to be right gives us the chance to change things. We don't necessarily need to break up in order to find a better relationship. Relationships are complex and there is likely something worth fighting for in yours. Many couples end up recovering and change. They find a way to be happy together even though all of their selfish needs aren't met all of the time. I would argue that the test of any successful marriage is if the couple will surrender to each other and find a way forward. If you are feeling a bit of panic, take a deep breath and keep reading; we will shortly discuss ways we can exit the world of right and realign our relationship trajectory.

7

Closing the Book on the World of Right

As we come to the end of this section, it might be tempting to think about the world of right as simply being an obstacle on the road to true happiness. "If only we could move this big rock out of the way, then it would be smooth sailing from here on out." The truth is a lot more shocking. It feels like the twist at the end of a great heist movie. The need to be right isn't just an obstacle along the path to happiness. It's the wrong path. We aren't even heading in the right direction.

I want to share with you the moment when I realized that I was trapped in the world of right.

It was a typical Friday night, and I was about to go on yet another first date. The process had been textbook. I'd found someone I wanted to take on a date, gotten the courage to ask her out, and—after enduring what seemed to be the longest week ever—finally arrived at the night of the date. We planned to go to dinner, get dessert, and just talk. Nothing too fancy.

Now normally it would take me about 30 minutes to get ready. But that night, I had spent about 2 hours finding the right shirt, doing my hair, redoing my hair, and changing my shirt. I was feeling nervous and anxious about the upcoming evening and I didn't know why. I was excited about the date, but my obsessive preening was going above and beyond for some reason. As I stopped to take one final look in the mirror, something occurred to me. I wasn't getting ready for my date; I was getting ready for myself. What I mean is that I was consumed with looking perfect because the date was about me, not about her. What I saw in that moment clarified the pattern I had been seeing in my other relationships. I had been dating only with myself in mind and never really seeing or connecting with others.

That night I realized I was living in the world of right, walking the wrong path to find dating happiness. When I was getting ready for all of those first dates, I was really trying to convince someone to come and play a part in my story. I wasn't actually committed to being happy. I wasn't open to the reality of others, I wasn't able to be authentic, and I was playing the very game I had so loudly bemoaned for so long. I was a hypocrite.

By now, you might think dating is a completely hopeless situation. But don't worry, not all is lost. In T.S Elliot's *The Cocktail Party*, Cecilia describes her distressed state of mind, saying, "I should really like to think there's something wrong with me—because, if there isn't, then there's something wrong… with the world itself—and that's much more frightening! That would be terrible. So, I'd rather believe there is something wrong with me, that could be put right" (Elliot, 1950). In the world of right, it seems that all problems and solutions lie outside of our control. This means change and improvement are not possible. In the world of happy, however, there is another way. The key to change is to recognize that we hold the key to change. It is something we can do right here and right now. Let's explore how we can do just that.

8

The World of Happy

This next part of the book is all about how we can learn to live in a different dating world—the world of happy. Pursuing "happy" means that dating works *for* us instead of against us. Instead of a competition to win the game and a frenzy to convince the best person to join our crusade, our desire to be happy is a collaborative pilgrimage toward a long and satisfying relationship. Our entire dating experience and subsequent relationships are transformed as we begin to choose a different way to approach and respond to others. From this new place, we see others as people and connect in ways we didn't know were possible. With these new eyes, we are ready to discover the gold that has been hiding under our feet.

What I love about striving to be happy is that it is very simple. We all have the skills, knowledge, and ability to enter this new world—one filled with connection, authenticity, love and (hopefully) dating success. The best part is, if we can start to walk the path of happy, not only are we more likely to find lasting love, but when we do, it will be based on a stronger foundation.

In the world of right we are focused on our story, filled with blame and resentment, and blind to our impact on other people. In the world of happy, we find the exact opposite. From this new place we become a person who is deeply interested in other people and their stories. We are curious, alive, and present with those we date. This new paradigm liberates us from needing to put on a show, and we are allowed to let our deeper self shine. In short, we can date authentically.

The potential results of living in the world of being happy are truly amazing. As we pursue happy, others find us more and more irresistible. They feel that we truly see them; they sense our good intentions. We reverse the polarity of our social magnet and, instead of pushing others away, we finally attract them to us. Nothing—not clothes, makeup, hair, car, money, body, degree, or anything you can do on the outside—is more attractive than someone who sees you, really listens to you, and desires you for who you are.

Our feelings also change in the world of happy. They draw us toward those with whom we might form the best connection. We still pursue those we are attracted to, but now we are able to see more clearly through the mist of confused emotions. We aren't rushed, stressed, or anxious because each date becomes an opportunity to get to know a new person who might one day become our partner.

In the world of happy, we seek to end the dating game. We are done with the specific rules and regulations governing how we approach people, or what to say, or the timing of things. We are concerned with and committed to finding a genuine connection with another human being and we, like a child learning to draw for the first time, color outside the lines.

When the ideas we have been discussing were first coming to mind, I discussed them with a single friend of mine. It was interesting, because when we started talking about the world of happy, his jaw clenched and his eyes narrowed. He did not like this idea. I was puzzled as to why. Shouldn't the world of happy come as a welcome respite in the stressful world of right? What I didn't realize then was that when I was talking about being happy, he was hearing the call of defeat. He was thinking that being happy meant to relinquish what he wanted, to give up, and settle. This couldn't be further from the truth. I want to be absolutely clear: being in love, finding someone who shares your values, being physically attracted to the person you are with, and finding happiness for yourself are all key to the world of happy. We are not going to dismiss these wonderful aspects of dating; we are simply going to allow them to flourish in the right way. Instead of clinging to our own version of happiness, we are open to being surprised. Instead of forcing what we want into existence through the deluded pursuit and manipulation of other people, we are going to let the vital components of love come alive the way they were meant to.

Living in the world of happy is about taking yourself *and* another person into account and writing your story together. Too often, I have seen people try to force their relationships to work without taking themselves into account. Being happy doesn't mean we forget about our experience and become a relationship martyr! You are an indispensable part of your relationships, and they are only successful to the extent that you are happy and cared for.

The world of happy is what dating was always meant to be. It unlocks the potential for an experience in dating that we didn't know was possible.

Trip to California

I want to tell you a story about an experience I had when dating my wife, Lizzie. About a month into our relationship, Lizzie went home to California for Christmas to visit her family. I thought it would be a romantic gesture if I visited, so I bought a plane ticket. I imagined that we would spend every day together and it was going to be nonstop fun.

The problem with this imaginary plan was that I had failed to consider that it was Christmas, one of the few times a year that Lizzie got to spend with her family. When I told her that I had purchased the ticket, she tried to warn me that she had very limited time to spend with me. I ignored her warnings, convinced everything would be great once I got to California.

I was wrong. Apart from three hours I was able to spend with her, I spent my nights watching movies alone at the theater, eating alone at a Denny's, and walking by myself along the beach. Did I mention that I was all alone? Needless to say, the trip was not turning out quite as I had hoped. I felt so stupid for having come in the first place and was about ready to give up. Note, I had all the red flags of needing to be right. I was telling a self-focused story, I was blind to my impact, and I was convinced that I wasn't the problem.

Then Sunday came around. I went to church with Lizzie and her family. After the service, I stood up to leave. As I made it to the door, I realized I was walking alone. When I looked back, I saw something that turned my whole experience on its head. It seemed like the entire congregation had lined up to see Lizzie. Seriously, it looked like a parade that culminated in a circle around her. Children, adults, old people—everyone was lining up to embrace her. She was a big deal in this community, and everyone loved her. I watched as she warmly embraced each person and with a kind smile took time to catch up with each of them. Time didn't seem to matter to her as she connected with these people she loved so much. This wasn't a unique moment for Lizzie, as I would come to find out. She is a warm and loving person to almost everyone she meets.

My entire trip, and perhaps my life, came into sharp focus in this moment as I watched her with these people. Time seemed to stop. I realized that she was a huge part of their lives. She was someone they cared about because she also cared for them. She was important on her own, and that importance was separate from what I was placing on her as my girlfriend. I could feel my list of needs and nopes being shredded as I *saw* her. She had so much going on—such great responsibilities and so much life to give. I saw her in terms of *her* for the first time in our short relationship and she was marvelous.

This realization turned my whole trip around. Instead of feeling sorry for myself for having wasted a week, all I could think about was how lovely Lizzie was and how much I wanted to spend more time with her. After this moment, I returned home and was filled with amazing energy and focus for my life. I could work hard. I could live life not gasping for air, but finally breathing it in. I was free from worrying about her place in my life because I saw her in hers, and she was amazing.

That experience snapped me out of my need to be right. It fundamentally changed my goals. I was now dating Lizzie in order to create a future together rather than just a life for myself. Lizzie can tell you how drawn she was to me after that moment. She felt that I really saw her and admired her for her own sake, not simply for *what* she was, but for *who* she was. This gave her the powerful invitation to commit to our relationship and see it through. I was finally striving to be happy *with* Lizzie, removing my self-focused barriers that had led to so much disappointment in my past relationships.

Now, it wasn't all sunshine and rainbows. I still had to untangle a very complicated knot that I had tied in the world of right. Even after we got engaged, I could feel waves of certainty and then waves of doubt. I felt strangely conflicted about committing to one person and wondered if maybe I could find someone better if I held out. Or if we had a disagreement, I would think maybe she wasn't the one. As I look back now, I can see clearly that these doubts weren't founded in any objective reality, they were the death rattles of the need to be right. I was mourning the death of *my* story. To commit to Lizzie meant that I needed to co-create with her. It required me to sacrifice parts of myself that I had built up in the world of right. She had to do the same and while the process was challenging at times, it was incredible how much stronger our relationship became.

I can tell you now that I absolutely made the right choice to marry Lizzie. While there are always challenges in a marriage, striving to be happy rather than right has blessed our relationship in a million ways.

Entering the World of Happy

Living in the world of happy sounds fantastic. But, like most things, it is much easier said than done. Alas, we can't just close our eyes, click our heels, and say, "I now want to be happy instead of right!" Like most things in life, it takes work and we have to start somewhere.

As we have learned from our own and others' experiences, we have developed three steps that might help you blaze a new trail toward the world of happy.

They are as follows:
Step 1. Consider other people.
Step 2. Be curious.
Step 3. Be helpful by being straightforward.

Let's dive in and see how this first step can help to open our hearts and minds to a new dating reality.

9

Step 1: Consider Other People

I want to propose something that might seem counter intuitive: moving forward by taking a step back. Instead of charging into dating with new ideas or techniques, I think it's most important to start by taking time to reflect on something fundamental. To take our first steps into the world of being happy, we need to open ourselves up to others and their reality. This means we need to start by taking others into account. Instead of pursuing a character to play in our production of "ME," we need to pursue a person who is a full human being and all that entails. Opening ourselves up to others allows us to change fundamentally the nature of our dating goals.

Lighting Up in the Cave

Several years ago, my friend Joe was set up on a blind double-date. The plan was to eat dinner and then explore a local cave. Joe had been looking forward to the date, but after a semi-awkward dinner, he felt let down that he wasn't particularly interested in or notably attracted to his date. If things continued in this same vein, Joe was worried that the caves wouldn't be any fun.

Upon arriving at the cave that evening, the group realized they had forgotten flashlights, and their cell phone batteries were low. Luckily, Joe had some glow sticks in the back of his truck, giving the couples just enough light to see their feet—barely. In reality, they were walking a quarter of a mile in complete darkness. The lack of light meant that each couple needed to depend on each other to navigate the precarious cave. Awkwardness gave way to jokes and giggling as each couple held hands and supported each other as they struggled to stand up on the icy floor and not hit their heads on the low roof of the cave. Suddenly, Joe found talking to his date a lot easier. She seemed to light up in the darkness of the cave. Soon, they were even flirting a bit. Joe thought to himself, "This girl is great! I totally misjudged her."

By the time they emerged from the caves, Joe's original opinion of his date had changed drastically. Even his level of attraction to her had increased significantly. When he dropped her off, the doorstep scene was easy because they were both having so much fun.

What happened to Joe summarizes exactly what it's like to take the first step in the world of happy. When Joe arrived for the date, he was only seeing the upcoming experience in terms of himself. When he met his date, she didn't fit into his plans the way he had hoped. The date turned a bit awkward as Joe's focus on himself sabotaged his ability to connect authentically. When they entered the dark cave, however, Joe suddenly needed to consider her wellbeing and connect with her. He forgot his one-sided story. He lost the fuel for his emotional pity party and was open to another person for the first time that night. When he finally opened himself up, he was surprised at what he found. His date was delightful and fun. It turned out they had similar interests. Joe experienced different emotions—emotions that propelled him toward her. She seemed to transform into a different person, when in reality, Joe was the one experiencing the transformation.

As They Really Are

To begin to consider other people in a way that will bring us toward the world of happy, we need to internalize something very important. Do you remember the greatest fear we have when we are living with a need to be right? It's the fear of settling. We are terrified we will end up with an ordinary someone who doesn't play the role we have written for them. When we enter the world of happy, we realize a core truth that we have been avoiding: there are no ordinary people.

This may seem obvious. But if you stop and think about it, it's a profound idea. There isn't a person that you know who is "ordinary" in the sense of not being unique or special in some way. Each person has their own contribution, their own skills, ideas, thoughts, fears, dreams, etc. Every single person we encounter has the potential to delight us, surprise us, or intrigue us in some way. Being open to another person is about acknowledging this truth and allowing it to affect how we see and approach them.

When we strive to live in the world of happy, we also recognize that people are imperfect. They have flaws, bad habits, and shortcomings; they make mistakes and, yes, fall short of our expectations at times. The truth, however, is that so do we. We acknowledge the fact that there is no perfect person, not even us. This understanding means that while we aren't going to settle, we are going to extend to others the grace we so fervently reserve for ourselves. This allows us to approach dating on even ground, accompanied by humility and gratitude. We can then get rid of assumptions and be open to the reality of another person.

I want you to take a moment with me. First, sit down and relax. Think about your life for just a moment. Think about how big and important your life is to you. Let your mind run with thoughts about your relationships, your work, how you have fun, and the many things you want to accomplish. Think of your unique background and story. Consider how nuanced and complex your life has become. Reflect on how important it all feels, how much your thoughts and opinions matter to you.

Now think about your hopes for the future. What do you hope for most in life? What are your greatest triumphs? Your greatest failures? What things about you are embarrassing? What things about you are likable? What do you fear? What have you learned and overcome through trial and error? Think about your hobbies and interests. Let your thoughts get lost in the grandeur of the mystery that is you.

Now think about how you matter to those you love. Think about those you love most. Who are they? Who do you interact with on a daily basis? Think of all the people to whom you have responsibilities. Seriously. Take five minutes, stop reading, and really contemplate all of it. If it helps, get a pen and paper and write down what comes to mind.

Now for the important part. While you're thinking about your big and crazy universe, I want you to think about someone else for just one moment. Perhaps it is the person you are dating, or maybe it's a stranger sitting across from you at the library. For right now, it doesn't matter who it is—just pick someone. Consider this incredibly simple truth: the person you are thinking about has a life that is just as full, crazy, complex, mysterious, quirky, embarrassing, and important as your own.

In fact, you have so much more in common with this person than you have differences. You both have goals, hopes, dreams, fears, and struggles. You both desperately want to be loved, appreciated, and recognized for the good things you do. You both want successful relationships and fulfillment. You both have minds filled with memories, opinions, thoughts, and ideas. Perhaps most sobering is that you both fear never finding true love and happiness. Take a moment to let the reality of the enormity of this person wash over you. Really stop and marinate in it. How does it feel? What do you realize? What is different now?

How did this exercise change the way you saw that person? Does it help you to appreciate them a bit more? Perhaps it helped paint them in a different light and now they aren't so intimidating. If you already liked them, do you feel more connected than before? Did you find that you have more in common with this person than you had previously realized? I hope it helped illuminate the fact that each person is more than just their superficial qualities. I hope it helps to ground the core truth that there are no ordinary people. People are amazing, and if we can simply remember that, we can create in ourselves a deep interest in them.

Above all, this exercise is meant to show us how much we don't know about other people. There are important aspects of others that we never explore because we are too focused on ourselves. Exposing our own ignorance allows us to break down these untrue assumptions about others that have been keeping us apart. What's more, it awakens a desire to know more; it helps us to become curious.

10

Step 2: Be Curious

Now that we have awakened a curiosity to know more about others by seeing how much we truly don't know, it's time to learn. If we are to see things clearly and begin to truly connect with others, we need to learn more about them. This is done through listening.

For this step, all you need to do is ask out someone that you'd like to learn more about. This can be anyone you feel comfortable with—a friend, colleague, or someone you're interested in dating. The goal on this date is simply to practice listening. You might even prep this person for the date by telling them that your goal is to listen to them. During this date, don't just hear their words; be present. Observe them, take in their presence, and allow yourself to be filled with a sense of wonder at their stories. Don't think up your own stories. Resist the impulse to jump in with your thoughts or opinions. Simply listen.

Prominent American journalist Brenda Ueland said about listening, "Listening is a magnetic and strange thing, a creative force.... When we are listened to, it creates us, makes us unfold and expand. Ideas actually begin to grow within us and come to life.... It makes people happy and free when they are listened to." When we listen, the dormant potential in us and in those around us comes to life. Brenda continues, "I discovered all this about three years ago, and truly it made a revolutionary change in my life. Before that, when I went to a party I would think anxiously: 'Now try hard. Be lively. Say bright things. Talk. Don't let up.' And when tired, I would have to drink a lot of coffee to keep this up. Now before going to a party, I just tell myself to listen with affection to anyone who talks to me, to be in their shoes when they talk; to try to know them without my mind pressing against theirs, or arguing, or changing the subject. No. My attitude is: 'Tell me more'...when I have this listening power, people crowd around and their heads keep turning to me as though irresistibly pulled" (Ueland, 1993).

Recently, experts conducted an interesting social experiment involving people who had never met before. The people were paired off and directed to ask each other a series of 36 very personal questions. Then, they simply listened as their partner responded. One of the participants reported, "The real crux of the moment was not just that I was really seeing someone, but that I was seeing someone really seeing me. Once I embraced the terror of this realization and gave it time to subside, I arrived somewhere unexpected" (Catron, 2015). After the experiment ended, some of the couples chose to go out with each other. A few of them even ended up in long-term relationships. Was it fate that brought them together? Perhaps. But a more likely explanation is that by listening to each other, they were able to lay the foundations of a successful relationship.

The magic of listening powerfully impacts our ability to bring our best and authentic self to dating. We feel liberated as we are lost in the other person. We no longer hear our internal voice telling us our own story. Listening unlocks our natural charm and intelligence. In place of self-consciousness, we find that we are comfortable in our own skin. We aren't intimidated or put off. We don't need to prepare the right answer, just the next question and that is given to us naturally by really listening. Each date becomes an adventure of discovery.

Imagine if dating were a game of listening rather than one of showing off. Wouldn't it be wonderful to learn about others more quickly and have clearer, more helpful information about those we are dating? We could make much better choices and waste less time trying to figure out how we feel. Our expectations would be properly tempered, offsetting disappointment. Our entire dating experience would be revolutionized into something enjoyable and enriching. The likelihood of finding long and lasting love would finally be more in our control.

Some worry that if they switch to listening, they will open themselves up to being hurt again. That by really seeing another person, they might too easily fall in love and/or risk exposure to those who would do them harm. Perhaps they fear that one more rejection will destroy their last semblance of self-confidence. Maybe they are tired of trying and feeling disappointed. Or they have been in toxic relationships in the past. Ultimately, they fear for the safety of their own hearts. These legitimate concerns are often raised by those who have experienced true heartache and sorrow. Here is my answer: when we are truly open to others and listen to them, we are finally able to see them clearly. We can make decisions grounded in reality instead of living in a fantasy we create in our mind. We can more accurately evaluate our own feelings. If there is any danger to be seen, we will be able to see and avoid it. We can more easily discover a true and lasting connection.

People might also ask, "What do I do if someone is not really listening to me?" It's a good question, one that I asked myself after a particularly frustrating date—the girl I'd gone out with had talked the entire time and not asked a single question about me. I returned from the date annoyed, slighted, and exhausted. My roommate saw I was bugged and asked what was wrong. He carefully listened as I told the story and then said, "Sam, just keep doing what you are doing. One day you will find someone who wants to be connected with."

His answer stunned me. He was absolutely right! In the world of being happy, our concern is not to make someone like us. Our concern is simply to keep ourselves open through trying to listen to others and trying to see them. It does not matter if they are ready to connect. What matters is that *we* are ready to connect, and when the time is right it will happen.

I challenge you to give it a try. Ask someone out or simply call them up and spend some time listening (30 minutes minimum). Like any skill, becoming a good listener is going to take practice. Clear your mind and open yourself up to whatever they are going to say. Learn all you can by asking questions. Go deeper than just the surface. Ask them why something is important to them, or what their point of view is. I have found that saying, "Tell me more about that" or "Why does that matter to you?" is a great way to expand a conversation beyond the routine first-date questions. Feel free to make a list of questions if this helps to keep you in the listening zone. There are great resources online and in other books that can give you plenty of question ideas (I will include a list of our favorite questions at the end of the book). You will be pleasantly surprised at what you learn as well as how much more connected and freer you feel. Who knows? Getting curious might just help that special someone feel seen by you, and that could lead to something great.

Now, I am aware that time is limited, especially for those of you reading with full-time work and other commitments. You might not have the time to finish all you have to do, let alone spend time listening to others for 30 minutes. I am also aware that online dating is now the norm for many, further reducing the amount of time you can spend with any one person. Don't get too hung up on the time, I want you to focus on the principle. Are you really listening when you do take time to go on dates (I mean *really* listening)? Are you present, awake, and focused on the person you are with? You can learn a lot in a short amount of time by forgoing the need to talk about yourself as you focus on listening to another person. Maybe taking more time to listen will actually help you be more efficient in your efforts to identify a great relationship.

Now don't worry, curiosity-oriented dates don't mean that we don't share about ourselves. In fact, by listening more, the other person is likely to want to listen to us. We get the chance to really be heard and seen. Curiosity sets the stage for the best flow of conversation and preps the ground for connection.

Once we consider that other people have a life that is just as big and important as our own, we naturally become more curious. We satisfy our curiosity and gain helpful clarity about others as we orient our dates to be more about learning than impressing. With this new information in mind, we are prepared to take control of our dating destinies and move on to Step 3.

11

Step 3: Be Helpful by Being Straightforward

Now that we have worked to see others and learn about them, it's time to take our newfound understanding and apply it. The third and final step of starting our journey in the world of happy is simply to be straightforward and honest.

Honest about what? Straightforward, how? It can be confusing when we are coming from the world of being right to see exactly what it means to be honest and straightforward. It can feel like we suddenly need to bare our souls to everyone we are dating, and that seems nuts. That's because it would be nuts and it's not what I am saying at all. When we think about being straightforward and honest in the world of happy, it's important to understand that this idea is ultimately grounded in our desire to form a lasting connection with another person. We are now dating with the serious goal of being happy long term and this means no more messing around. Gone are the days of waffling back and forth and refusing to commit to a direction.

This might appear daunting, but remember, by arriving at Step 3, we have already taken time to consider the reality of others and learn more about those we are dating. This means that we now have a clearer picture of the person we are interested in. We can now see whether they are someone we want to pursue, just be friends, or break off the connection altogether. Regardless of the direction we choose to take, it is more likely to be the right one for both parties. With this understanding in hand, it's time to tell the truth about our feelings and set the stage for a connection to either form or dissipate. Either way, by communicating our intentions straightforwardly and honestly, we will save time, reduce confusion, and get the ball rolling in the right direction.

Yikes. Being straightforward, upfront, and honest with those we date seems terrifying. This is because in the world of right, we are committed to carefully keeping the dating game rules. These rules consist of a strict set of dos and don'ts that must be adhered to in order to be considered cool/savvy. No texting right after the date, don't date people who you work with, or attend school or church with, and don't tell them how you feel too fast or you'll seem desperate. You might have heard that you shouldn't talk to someone you like in person at first but follow them on Instagram, like something they posted, and then DM them before approaching them. The rules are always changing but the game is the same: try to convince someone to like you.

I, for one, would love to end this dating game, wouldn't you? Think about it. Wouldn't it be great if those who liked us would tell us? How about if those whom we date let us know when they're not happy before the whole thing goes up in smoke? What would it be like to have others be upfront about their thoughts, feelings, and intentions? This would improve our communication and make things far less awkward. We would stop leading people on or toying with their emotions. All of the benefits, just one price—being straightforward and honest, always with the goal to be helpful.

The Pitfalls of Not Being Straightforward

Theoretically, we all know that dishonesty negatively impacts others. I learned about this firsthand when I started going out with a girl near my apartment. We'd gone out a few times, but after several weeks, I didn't really feel like dating her. But I didn't want to hurt her feelings by telling her—I was a nice guy, after all! So, I let things just continue.

One night, I was sitting in my apartment, telling a few friends about how I didn't want to date this girl. A few minutes into the conversation I got a text from the girl herself saying that if I didn't want to date, I should have just told her! Turns out she had come over to say hi, but before she had come into the apartment, she had heard me talking with my friends about her. Oh man, I really screwed that one up!

What would have been most helpful to her in this situation? Being honest and straightforward. Instead, I had been more committed to looking like a good guy than actually helping her. My cowardice, motivated by my need to be right, deeply hurt her and embarrassed me. She could have moved on much earlier or have been spared the disappointment if I had simply told her the truth instead of talking behind her back. Lesson learned: honesty is helpful!

Too often, however, people are more committed to looking good (not being the bad guy) than being helpful and honest. Or they are worried that if they tell the other person the truth about their feelings toward them that the other person will get scared and run away. Here is the cold truth: if we are honest about our feelings and the other person responds poorly, that is on them. Our honesty releases us and them from the chaos and captivity created by ambiguity, and even if they can't see it yet, provides both parties a much better way forward.

In the end, dishonesty leads to bad relationships drawn out, love unspoken, opportunities missed, and messy breakups. So much of this pain can be avoided if we acknowledge the truth by being straightforward and honest.

What Honesty Looks Like

Now, I'm not saying that being straightforward and honest is a license to be a jerk or a creeper. Honesty is not about breaking hearts, and it's not an excuse to profess love to everyone we meet. In practice, being straightforward means that we are open and honest with the person we are dating every step of the way. We try to be honest about who and where we are. We don't start our relationships with big talks or drama. We simply live authentically, and when the moments are right, we have straightforward dialogue about our thoughts and feelings. For example, we might be on a second date and feel it would be right to let someone know we enjoy spending time with them and would like to do more of it. Or we might be six weeks into a relationship and feel it's time to end it. It might be time to set boundaries for someone who has been pursuing us, or to take a moment to ask out someone we want to spend more time with. Basically, we genuinely try our best to express what we really think and feel and give the other person license to do the same.

When we are honest and straightforward, we are more concerned with being helpful and connected to another person rather than spending any amount of time in the fantasy world of being right. We want others to know how we feel so they can honestly evaluate their own feelings. We set a clear, straight course toward what we want, allowing us to find those who share our vision.

Keep in mind the order of the steps. If we skip Step 1 (considering others) and Step 2 (being curious), we won't have the information we need for Step 3 (being honest and straightforward). If we dive straight into honesty without learning about the other person, we might do more harm than good! First we need to take the time to see someone and learn about them. Once we have a grasp on the relationship and who they are, we can offer honest feedback. Sometimes this happens quickly; in other cases, it may take more time. Our goal with Step 3 is to foster honest communication, creating an environment in which love can blossom.

Straightforward Versus Forward

Please note that there is a big difference between being straightforward and being forward. They might seem similar at first glance, but straightforward and forward are born out of completely different goals. When we are straightforward, we are simply looking at the truth and speaking it. Being forward, on the other hand, means pushing things along at an unreasonable pace. Forward people are more committed to their timeline than to honoring the feelings of the other person.

When my wife and I first met and started spending time together, I sensed that she didn't feel for me what I was feeling for her. One night after hanging out, I felt strongly that if I didn't act soon, I would be doomed to the relationship purgatory we call "the Friend Zone." I decided that instead of going quietly into love jail, I would stage a coup by trying to be honest with her. I called her up and invited her over for a quick chat. When she arrived, I sat her down and said "Listen, I really like hanging out with you, but I am feeling like you might be tempted to friend-zone me. Which is fine, by the way. However, I can't let you friend-zone me without knowing that I really like you and I am interested in dating you. If that's not cool with you, that is alright. We can just be friends and we don't have to keep our taco date for Wednesday." Lizzie just sat there in stone cold silence for a solid minute (which killed me). She then said "Wow, that was super brave... so I guess we are still on for tacos?" That was code for, she heard me and was willing to take another step. I just smiled and said, "That sounds perfect, I can't wait."

Can you see the difference here? I wasn't trying to be forward. I wasn't expecting her to reciprocate. I was simply honest about where I was and gave her the information she needed to make a choice. I didn't want to waste time. I didn't want to play the game any longer. If she had friend-zoned me, that would have been just fine. No matter how that conversation went it would have provided clarity. As it was, this short conversation put the relationship into another gear. We were free to move forward more quickly and openly. By being honest and straightforward with each other we were on the path to building a happy future together.

Step 3 Action Plan

The action piece of Step 3 is simple. Choose someone specific, then run through Steps 1 and 2 with them. Once you have a clearer understanding of this person, take a moment to look deep inside yourself and ask, "If I were being helpful and committed to happiness for myself and this person, what would I need to do?" And then go do it.

Maybe it's admitting you were wrong and apologizing. Perhaps it's finally telling someone that you have feelings for him or her. It could be time to end that relationship or let that person know that you're not interested. Or maybe it's time to give them a chance! Perhaps you need to go out of your way to help them with a project. Maybe you feel you should spend more time with this person. Whatever you feel, start doing it. You will immediately notice a sense of confidence and feel liberated from the tension caused by not expressing or doing what you feel you should do.

You will be blown away at how quickly the other person responds to being treated this way. Often, they will respond in kind and offer their own help and honesty. It is possible that they don't reciprocate or even respond poorly. That is okay. What is the alternative? Do we go back to the days of playing the game and all the ridiculous rules? No way! Screw the rules! So what if the other person's response isn't what you hoped for?! At least you will have given it your best and you can be free to move on without regrets. Being straightforward and honest is a great way to weed out those who are not in a place to connect.

Step 3 requires courage—the courage to be helpful by being straightforward and honest. But know that the payoff is great.

12

How Will I Know?

How do I know I have found the one?! This might be the most urgent and common question asked by singles. It's an important question and one that has different answers depending on your goals.

If we are living in the world of right, the answer is: when my story makes sense. When I have finally checked the boxes and tracked down a successful, attractive, and likable partner. When I have feelings that coincide with the romantic stories I have heard or have had some experience that proves that I am making the right choice.

If we are living in the world of happy, the answer is: when we find a great relationship. How can we know what a great relationship looks like? Now that we've torn up our "need" and "nope" lists (you did tear them up, right?), what should we be looking for? I believe that every great relationship includes some combination of the following components.

#1. Mutual Admiration: Admiration is defined by a warm respect for another person. It's something that is usually based on qualities that are more substantial than just physical attraction. We might find ourselves admiring someone's intelligence or their kindness, their optimistic outlook or maybe the way they help others. They might be a great listener or a conversationalist. Whatever it is, finding qualities that we admire is key if we are to fortify a relationship for the long haul. Admiration is one of the first things we should filter for when searching for true love.

#2. Common Values: Values are core beliefs about what is important in life and how we should live. Walking the journey of life with someone who is aligned in this deep way makes everything easier and more likely to be successful. Because starting from common ground breeds better communication, a relationship built on common values is more resilient through many of life's challenges.

#3. Trust: Take a moment and imagine the kind of relationship you would like to be in long term. Maybe the word "marriage" or "partnership" comes to mind. Whatever you are thinking about, I can guarantee you that at the core of any ideal relationship you will find trust. Imagine what it would be like to be committed to someone who had a hard time telling you the truth? When it comes down to it, if we are going to form a strong and lasting relationship it has to be built on a foundation of trust.

#4. Fun: One of the best indications of a great relationship is if you have fun together. Think about your best friends; I bet they are people you have fun with. Not only does it make life more enjoyable, but it's also a core ingredient in the forming of joyful memories. Fun is an antidote to many of life's inevitable troubles and something that makes the journey together wonderful. Pay attention to the people you have fun with as they might be great candidates for a long-lasting relationship.

#5. Work Ethic: Finding someone who will work on your relationship with you is vital. Life will throw all sorts of curveballs at you, and someone who is willing to work to make a relationship better and stronger is a true partner. Many successful couples report feeling "lucky" to have found one another. I have seen that what they mean is that they feel grateful to have a partner who doesn't back down in the face of relationship challenges and sticks with them through thick and thin. You can know if someone has this relationship work ethic by looking at their other relationships. Do they take time with the people they love? Do they think about and try to improve the lives of those in their life? Do they thrive on drama or try to make peace? From your side, you can ask yourself, "Is this someone I want to fight for and with to make the future brighter?" If so, then you, too, are "lucky" in love.

These five components are not the only qualities that make up a great relationship, they are simply good indicators that might help you discover one. The key is to stay open and search for those things that will lead you toward fulfilling the goal of being happy. There is no need to make lists; just pay attention to those things that matter most.

Breaking Up in the World of Happy

Even when we are striving to be happy, not all relationships will work out. That is okay. We still have to do and experience hard things—and in dating, breaking up is one of the hardest. Luckily, when our goal is happiness, we can get through these moments in a much more helpful way.

Mark and Jenny

About four months after Mark started dating Jenny, he felt it was time to end the relationship. He had liked Jenny at first, but now he genuinely felt that it was time to move on so they could both find someone else.

Mark decided he would be straightforward and honest with her, starting by having the difficult conversation right away instead of putting off the breakup like he had felt tempted to do. He explained how he felt about the relationship. He told her that he did not feel about her the way she deserved; he couldn't see a future for them, and he wanted to end the relationship. He apologized briefly to her for any pain this would cause. He then gave her a chance to express her feelings and ask questions.

Jenny was upset, of course, as no one likes being broken up with. But as they talked, they both realized this was not a relationship they were committed to fixing. When the conversation was coming to an end, Mark told Jenny that she could choose how she wanted their relationship to be from now on. If she wanted to be friends, that was fine. If not, that was fine too. He was going to stay away for a bit, but if she wanted to talk or be friends, he would be available.

Later, Jenny told Mark that she had never been broken up with in such a straightforward way. She explained that, while it hurt to lose him, his approach had freed her from resentment and confusion, and she was able to move on almost right away.

Rachel and Tim

Rachel went through a very different sort of breakup. She and Tim had been dating for a year. She loved him deeply and was sure they were going to get married. Even up until the very end, it felt like he felt the same way. The week before the breakup, he had taken her to a family reunion, bought her an expensive gift, and told her he loved her.

Just days after returning from the family reunion, however, the bomb dropped. He didn't want to keep dating. When Rachel asked him how long he had felt this way, he said it had been a little more than a month. A month?! How could he have continued to pretend that he loved her with these doubts in his heart? Why did he let things drag on? She had just met his family, for crying out loud! Needless to say, she felt betrayed and lied to.

Their breakup was not a pretty one. During their conversation, he cried for a couple of hours over how guilty he felt. He went on and on about how wonderful she was and how he just couldn't get himself to take the next steps and commit. He was adamant that he was heartbroken too, and he insisted that he would never find someone like her again. Imagine Rachel's dismay when a friend called to report that Tim's profile was back up on a popular dating app the very next day. Rachel wished that Tim had simply told her of his misgivings earlier. Perhaps they could have fixed things, or at least ended things earlier without so much emotional wreckage.

Let's break down these two breakups to see what we can learn.

It seems Mark was striving to be happy and to make sure that Jenny was able to be happy as well. Mark knew that continuing in the relationship would have been wrong. Instead of trying to preserve Jenny's feelings and bolster his own virtue, Mark simply stated what he felt and what he planned to do and then allowed her the space and time to work through it herself. He didn't wait too long to tell her of his feelings. He didn't patronize her with false praise or manipulate her experience. He allowed her to set the terms of their friendship after the breakup. He wanted to make sure that he was true to her and himself. His honesty and helpfulness allowed Jenny to move on without feeling broken, helping her to be in the best possible spot for when she met and found her now-husband.

Compare that to Tim's breakup. It seems to me that Tim was breaking up while needing to be right. He was trying to find a way to feel like a good person while being dishonest and then moving on as quickly as possible. His self-focused approach deeply hurt Rachel. She felt deceived and manipulated. What's more, she lost confidence in herself for future relationships. Don't worry, Rachel has since married an incredible guy, and recently gave birth to a beautiful baby girl.

When the Answer Is No

What about when we are the one being broken up with or rejected? People can have intense reactions to rejection, especially when it comes to matters of the heart—they may become hurt, offended, and even angry. Others refuse to accept "no" and continue to try even when there is no hope. Personally, I think the way we respond to rejection is a great litmus test for whether we want to be right or happy. If we are looking to be right, rejection is like a shattering of our universe. This other person is wrecking the future we have built for ourselves, and all our unrealistic hopes are dashed. If we are filled with feelings of anger, offense, or despair, perhaps we were more committed to our own story and have been ignoring the needs of the other person.

Instead of interpreting rejection as a crushing blow, however, we can see it in a different way. When we see and honor the feelings of others, we realize that their reasons for rejecting us are entirely their own. This ultimately spares us from the awful feelings we have come to associate with breakups and dating. It doesn't mean it's going to be a walk in the park, but we *can* remove our own offended feelings, which will change our experience. When our goal is to be happy, we can honor the wishes of the other person, accept rejection with grace, and perhaps move on more quickly to find a relationship with someone who will reciprocate our feelings.

It's important to point out that searching for happiness doesn't mean we will always find it. Often, we are required to go through difficult moments, including heartbreak, rejection, dashed hopes, and dating droughts, to name a few. But when we are trying to be happy, we are able to approach these troublesome times with greater clarity, giving us the perspective needed to move forward. As my freshmen psychology professor said, "Happiness is the byproduct of living a true life. It does not mean we will always be happy, but when we are happy, it will be true."

13

Final Thoughts On the World of Happy

The three steps we talked about are not just a one-and-done deal. They represent a pattern of living and perceiving that you can apply to every relationship at any level. As you embrace this way of life, you may be surprised by how much more fulfilling your relationships can be.

Let's take one last look at the three steps to living in the world of happy.

1. Consider other people—see the truth about others.
2. Be curious—truly listen to learn.
3. Be helpful by being straightforward.

Each of these steps leads to the other, so simply start with Step 1. They are especially effective at helping a new relationship get off to a great start. And if you are already in a relationship with someone, these steps will further improve it.

Ultimately, this process is designed to help change our underlying goal of needing to be right. As we shift our goal, our thoughts and actions will change. We will stop trying to be right and simply start trying to do what is right. The desire to be helpful will become natural to us, and our dating experiences and results will be transformed.

I want to call attention to something important. Notice that the three steps to entering the world of happy have nothing to do with changing your appearance, your "game," your career, your personality, or your preferences. You can be an introvert, an extrovert, or any combination of -vert and still pursue the goal of being happy. It doesn't matter what has happened to you in your dating past, whether you have been successful or not, or even if you have been previously married. I don't care what Hogwarts house the Facebook quiz sorted you into—absolutely everyone can start to date in this new and refreshing way. Entering the world of happy does not mean changing anything about what makes you *you*. It's all about changing the underlying goal and how we see and approach other people.

So much dating advice you will find from friends, family, online, or other books will direct you to alter some part of who you are in order to increase your desirability. Sometimes this advice is needed or well intentioned. If you don't have a habit of showering or brushing your teeth, you might want to start. Unfortunately, too much of what constitutes "dating advice" is founded in the world of right and is enticing because it provides a supposed way to accomplish our superficial and self-focused goals. Being happy is a different approach altogether and one that will guide us to those who will truly love us for the long haul.

Life has a funny way of opening the next chapter only when we are ready for it. I know this was true in my case. As soon as I began trying to live in the world of happy, I met my wife. Dating her was unlike any experience I had had before. It could be said that I had finally found the "one," and perhaps that is true. However, my courtship with Lizzie wasn't free from challenges. I believe I was simply better equipped to commit to a relationship because my goal was no longer to protect my self-interest. For the first time in my dating life, I was ready to make a connection, and, as a result, love blossomed.

The Right Foundation

The best part about the world of happy is that all your problems are solved and whoever you choose to marry will love you forever and nothing will go wrong... Of course, I'm kidding, but I was just checking that you are still with me.

Living in the world of happy does not exempt us from challenges, even when we find true and lasting love. The good news is that when we do find that long-term partner, we have started the relationship on much more solid ground. We are living in a way that allows us to see clearly and avoid creating roadblocks to helping love thrive. We live without the toxic expectations that come from trying to force our self-focused story into reality. Our partner can shine on their own, make their own choices, change, grow, excel, outshine us, and thrive beyond our preconceived notions. Our goal of being happy ultimately uplifts and enriches our partner in a way that invites them to reciprocate and bless us with the same.

Our daily life in a long-term, committed relationship in the world of happy is also better oriented to resist conflict and miscommunication. The approach of considering the other person's point of view and becoming curious about them lends itself to a communication style that is kind and patient. If the other person disagrees, we don't see them as a threat to our objectives, but simply as a person with a different view. This allows us to apply grace and accommodate their input better into our discussions and decision-making process.

You can probably see more application for both the world of right and the world of happy when it comes to different relationships. Parents and children, co-workers, extended family, communities, churches, etc. My hope in applying these ideas to dating is that we can begin better marriages. This will lead to stronger families, more love, and a better society overall.

Do you remember Jordan from the beginning of the book? He also applied these ideas to his career and discovered that he was on the wrong track. He realized that his career choices were being governed by the story he wanted to tell about himself. He was able to question his story even further and decided to abandon his pursuit of a position in academia. He and his wife now own a business together and he reports never having been happier. Now it's your turn, I invite you to apply these ideas to different arenas and see what happens.

Note: it is easy once these ideas have been understood to see the need to be right in others and the desire to be happy in ourselves. If you want to offend someone, then I recommend trying to convince them that they are needing to be right. Always remember that the need to be right, like the desire to be happy, is very personal. Try your best to only apply the ideas to how you date and don't use them to blame others or exalt yourself. Keep in mind, our example is the most powerful way to help others change. Keeping things in the proper frame will help to make these ideas truly effective in any place you choose to apply them.

The Choice is Yours

The choice is yours: you can be right, or you can be happy. If you choose to be right, then no matter how you try, happiness will elude you. You will alienate the very people you are trying to attract, create barriers, and find yourself feeling disappointed with dating. Or worse, it could lead to relationships built on self-interest. If you choose the world of happy, you will find the key to unlocking greater success in your dating endeavors and build the foundation of lasting love.

I wish you, reader, the best of luck. Please don't feel overwhelmed. Simply take things step by step. It has been said that the canyon is carved out one drop of water at a time. It is already inside each of us to live in the world of being happy. All we need to do is start. So why not today?

14

Appendix:

Questions to Ask on a Date/Becoming a Better Listener

Here are some questions that you can use when on a date to put you in the listening seat and give you greater insight into those you're dating. You might use one or two of these to kick off a conversation. You could also make a date of asking all 20 questions. Whatever you choose to do, these questions are here to help you develop the habit of listening.

1. What is something good that has happened to you lately?
    - Why are you excited about it?
    - What does it mean for your future?
2. If I could give you a billion dollars, what would you do with it?
    - What experiences have you had that influenced why you said what you did?

3. What are some qualities that you admire in other people?
    - How about in yourself?
    - Tell me more about that.
4. What is something that you wish other people would recognize about you?
    - Why do you think they don't?
5. Can you tell me about when you had the most fun you've ever had?
    - Why was it so much fun for you?
6. If you could travel the world with one person from history, who would it be and why?
    - Where would you go on your trip?
7. Do you have a best friend?
    - Why is this person your best friend?
8. What did you want to be when you were little?
    - How does your life path now match that little person's dreams?
9. What is something you worry about?
10. What do you find yourself thinking about when you have free time?
    - Why do you think that is coming up for you?
11. What is something about you that you think others would find embarrassing?
12. Have you ever had your heart broken?
    - If you're willing to share, how has that experience shaped you?
13. Tell me about your parents. What are they like?

- What about them do you hope you can keep doing?
- What about them do you hope not to repeat?
14. Have you ever eaten anything that changed your life?
15. What is your go-to memory when you want to feel happy?
    - Why this memory?
16. What would you consider to be the biggest adventure you have had in your life so far?
17. If you had to leave lessons behind for future generations, what would they be?
    - What experiences have you had that make you say what you said?
18. If your life were a telenovela, what would you include as the weird twist?
19. What do you hope to accomplish with your dating journey?
20. If you could solve one world problem right now, what would it be and why?

Tips for Being Straightforward and Honest:

The following are ideas or prompts to help you get started with having 3 kinds of conversations that you might need to have:

1. Telling someone you like them.
2. Breaking up with someone.
3. Letting someone down who likes you.

Please take these with a massive grain of salt and keep in mind that they are just ideas. You ultimately get to choose who you approach and what is the best way to go about it.

It is important to keep in mind that what others will respond to most is not what you say, or even how you say it, but your deeper motivations. If you are approaching someone with the intent to manipulate or change them, they will feel it. If, however, you are looking to be honest and helpful then they will feel that too. Take time before you start this process to run through Steps 1–2 from the second half of this book to ensure you are seeing clearly and have the right information before endeavoring to have these potentially tough conversations.

Telling someone you like them

Telling someone you like them in the world of happy is fairly simple. It takes courage to say it, but even more courage to simply let the chips fall where they will. Remember, we aren't telling someone we like them to force them to confess their love for us. We don't expect anything in return. We are simply being honest because that is how we want to define our relationships. Here is an example of how you might open up a conversation to tell someone you like them.

- "Honesty is super important to me and so I want to tell you how I feel about you. I like you. I really enjoy being around you and I want to keep getting to know you better to see where things could go. Would you be open to going out with me (or continue going out with me)? If not, no problem, I just wanted to be sure you were clear on where I am."

Breaking up with someone

When breaking up with someone, it can be so tempting to try and soften the blow. We want to manage the other person's feelings and how they see us. Remember, the other person is a person. This means that they are responsible for managing their own feelings. You cannot and should not try to control their response or manipulate them. This is why I advocate for a straightforward and quick breakup.

- "I know it might come as a shock, but I can't continue to date you. I feel that we both need to move on. If you would like to stay friends, that is great, but I will give you space until you decide. I am so sorry."

The other person will likely want to find out why you are breaking up with them. I suggest being honest about your feelings without accusing them or bringing up their faults. Simply and clearly state that you feel that it's not the right relationship for you and that you need to move on.

Avoid telling them they are amazing or wonderful; this contradicts what you are doing. There is no need to complement or degrade them; you are talking about your experience only.

If the person begins to try and talk you out of the breakup, it's time to hold firm and walk away. Reiterate that you're not feeling committed to the relationship and that you want to move on. I know this might seem strange or cold at first, but there is nothing the person can say that will change your mind. In fact, even though they might not see it, you are trying to be compassionate by not feeding into their own need to be right. By staying true to yourself in this crucial moment, you will free both you and them from unnecessary emotional struggle.

Letting down someone who likes you

Letting someone down can be difficult. Like breaking up, we could feel the need to manage their feelings. You might consider something like this:

- "Thank you for the compliment; I am so flattered that you like me. I do not feel the same about you. I am sorry if this hurts your feelings. I want to be honest so both of us can move forward."

The other person may try to convince you otherwise or ask you to give them a chance. You can follow that up with a simple "no."

Preparing what you need to say

Notice the three essential components of each example. These components can be used to improve your communication and help you prepare what you need to say.

1. I use "I" statements, not "you" statements. I am not trying to accuse the other person. Accusing someone will put up their defenses and make the conversation much harder.
2. The sentences are concise. I don't want to beat around the bush. Long and drawn-out explanations complicate our communication and put at risk the objective of the conversation.
3. The message is clear. Each sentence is calculated to communicate exactly what I need and give the other person the most necessary information. I don't have to worry about getting the message across and the other person isn't left guessing.

THANKS FOR READING

VISIT OUR WEBSITE

- Free Tools
- Coaching
- Book a Speaker
- Join our Newsletter

www.rightorhappybook.com

Acknowledgments

- My friends, family and beautiful wife for putting up with all the asks and editing. This book exists because of you.
- A big thank you to Zach Kristensen for being my excellent publishing coach. He helped me through the complex world of self-publishing. If you would like a worldclass publishing coach, check out his website: www.juxtabook.com
- Thank you to Mel Wise who helped me with the cover design. They were wonderful to work with.
- Chapter images from:
  1. Designed by rawpixel.com / Freepik
  2. Rochak Shukla through www.freepik.com
  3. www.freepik.com
     1. Camera rawpixel.com
     2. Typewriter rawpixel.com
     3. Eye glasses rawpixel.com
     4. Balloon child Rochak Shukla
     5. Compass rawpixel.com
     6. Divers helmet rawpixel.com
     7. Binoculars rawpixel.com
     8. Horse Jump Rochak Shukla
     9. Quill and ink rawpixel.com
     10. Key rawpixel.com
     11. Lock Free Pik
     12. Key 2 Free Pik
     13. Checklist Free Pik
     14. Vintage phone Free Pik
     15. Vintage clock Free Pik
     16. Umbrella Free Pik

17. Mask Free Pik
18. LightHouse Free Pik
19. Candle Free Pik

References

Bosker, B. (2019). *HuffPost is now a part of Oath.* Huffpost.com. Retrieved June 4, 2019, from https://www.huffpost.com/entry/tinder-experiment_n_3077047

Catron, M. (2015). *To fall in love with anyone, do this.* Nytimes.com. Retrieved June 4, 2019, from https://www.nytimes.com/2015/01/11/fashion/modern-love-to-fall-in-love-with-anyone-do-this.html?smid=fb-nytimes&smtyp=cur&bicmp=AD&bicmlukp=WT.mc_id&bicmst=1409232722000&bicmet=1419773522000&_r=0

Eliot, T. S. (1950). *The cocktail party.* Ecco.

Marcel Proust quotes. (n.d.). BrainyQuote.com. Retrieved March 9, 2020, from https://www.brainyquote.com/quotes/marcel_proust_137794

Real, B., Bertot, J. C., & Jaeger, P. T. (2014). Rural public libraries and digital inclusion: Issues and challenges. *Information and Technology Libraries, 33*(1), 6–24.

Santayana, G. (1982). *Reason in common sense.* Dover Publ,

Ueland, B. (1993). *Strength to your sword arm: Selected writings.* Holy Cow! Press.

Warner, C. T. "The Hidden Spiritual Character of Psychological Healing." The Arbinger Institute, 2001.

www.ingramcontent.com/pod-product-compliance
Lightning Source LLC
Chambersburg PA
CBHW070148080526
44586CB00015B/1889